Big Al's
How To Build MLM Leaders
For Fun & Profit

by
Tom Schreiter

KAAS Publishing
P.O. Box 890084
Houston, TX 77289

http://www.fortunenow.com

Phone: (281) 280-9800
Fax: (281) 486-0549

Printed in the United States of America

Copyright © 1991 by KAAS Publishing

ISBN 1-892366-03-7

Cover Design: Mark Cummings

Illustrations: Mark Cummings

About the Author

Tom "Big Al" Schreiter has a knack for seeing the obvious, and projecting inaccurate conclusions. While many MLM leaders have taken the safe, logical and sure path to success, Tom insists on exposing most MLM "truths" as misleading myths.

Tom is a charter member of WWT (Writers Without Talent) and winner of the Webster, TX "Survival of the Fattest" competition.

Commercial Plug:

If you have read his other four books (*Sponsoring Magic: Big Al Tells All, How To Create A Recruiting Explosion, Turbo MLM,* and *Super Prospecting: Special Offers & Quick-Start Systems*), you'll certainly enjoy this volume.

Table of Contents

Cloning superhuman leaders

Distributors come and go. It's how many MLM leaders you have that count. Your strength, security, and income depend on the number of leaders in your group, not on the number of transient distributors passing through.

How many leaders does it take to make you financially successful? One can do it. Many, many successful MLMers earn $5,000, $10,000, $15,000 a month and more in bonus overrides from just one good productive downline leader. So, if you had a career choice, what would you choose . . .

1. Look, locate, or build a single successful MLM leader who will earn you thousands per month in bonus overrides?

or,

2. Spend the rest of your MLM career hustling to replace transient distributors to keep your bonus check above minimum wage?

The choice is easy. Find, locate, train, build or whatever you have to do to get one successful MLM leader in your downline.

An ancient conqueror once said, "If I lose my entire army of 100,000 men, no problem. As long as I have 10 good leaders, I can rebuild my army quickly. If I lose my 10 good leaders, my 100,000 army will be useless and will quickly disperse."

Sounds like having leaders is a pretty good deal.

The smart MLM superstars have several MLM leaders in their downline. And their life is easy.

For example, when the MLM superstar goes to Hawaii for vacation, he doesn't have to worry about the weekly opportunity meeting. One of his downline leaders will take responsibility for meeting set-up, registration table, etc. The downline leader doesn't care if the upline leader even attends. He wants to build his own downline for his own personal reasons. He doesn't need upline prodding or motivation. In fact, this is a great time for the downline leader to show off his responsibility and effectiveness.

Now, try going to Hawaii with only transient distributors in your downline. You have to call back daily to solve a mini-crisis, check on product delivery, find out if anyone will attend the meeting, and hope your weekly opportunity meeting doesn't turn out to be an opportunity meeting for the competition. If you don't have downline leaders in your MLM group, you can never rest.

Well, if having MLM leaders is best, how do you go about getting one?

Choice #1 is to find a MLM leader with the competition and convince him to come over to your team. It's easy and simple. Just promise him a better deal. This is the quick, painless way to get a leader fast. There is no investment in training. No long waiting time for your leader to develop. And, your new leader probably has an instant downline he can persuade to take with him.

Only one little problem. If you can persuade this leader to come to your team by offering a better deal, won't your new leader be prey to your competition offering an even better deal to steal him away from you?

In bars across the U.S., men discuss the nature of marriage. The sage advice is: Never steal another man's wife. If she will cheat on her husband to eventually marry you, guess what? Now you are her husband and what will happen to you?

Women already know this logic and don't have to go to bars for instruction.

So, if you think you can take a shortcut and steal leaders from the competition, then you will end up with leaders always open to better offers to leave your organization. Not a very comforting and secure thought.

Choice #2 is to home-grow your leaders. That means to take someone with the desire to succeed and invest your time to give him the skills to be a successful MLM leader. It takes time. It won't happen overnight. And you may find that your choice really doesn't have the commitment and desire to develop into that responsible MLM leader, your next superstar. You may have to invest in several potential MLM leaders to get your superstar.

How do you build them? Commitment. Here's how one MLM leader builds a superstar every year.

First, he finds a distributor with unbelievable desire. Maybe this distributor has no skills, is rough around the edges, and has a long, long way to develop. But that's not important. What is important is desire.

Second, the MLM leader gets a long-term commitment from his distributor. He makes sure the distributor sees the vision and understands the commitment and investment the MLM leader is making in him. With the MLM leader as his mentor, the distributor is almost guaranteed MLM success and financial riches.

Third, the work begins. The MLM leader/mentor becomes the distributor's constant companion. They do two-on-one presentations together. They split duties at the opportunity meetings. They split duties at the training meetings and regional rallies. They go on the road together. For the next six months they'll look like Siamese twins.

At the end of six months the distributor knows everything that his upline leader knows PLUS whatever skills, knowledge and talents that the distributor possesses in addition to his upline's training. The distributor knows everything his upline leader does PLUS more! A new, more powerful leader has been developed, one that surpasses his mentor.

Now, how would you feel to have a downline leader with even more talent, knowledge and skills than you personally possess? Not only is it a good feeling, it's a profitable feeling. How would you feel to have a downline of 10 superstars, each with greater ability than yourself? Rich, very rich.

Cloning more downline leaders is even easier. When you have invested your six months (or even a year) in your first leader, you now can go on to build leader #2. Your first-level leader can go on to build another leader also. If you mentored correctly, your first leader will follow your slow, sure, methodical building technique that guarantees success.

And his leaders will be even better than yours. Why? Your second-level leader will learn everything that you know, plus everything your first-level leader taught him, PLUS every additional talent, knowledge or skill he already has. Now that's powerful. It's like building second generation super-human leaders. It's profitable too.

Why does this cloning or mentor technique work so well? Because it is self-perpetuating. Let's say you have ten downline distributors. You announce that distributor #1, John, has made a commitment to be an MLM leader. The other nine distributors nod in agreement and say, "That's nice." John and you are becoming partners for the next six months of leadership training. They understand that 80% of your time will be spent with John, and the remaining time to meet their lesser commitments.

Now picture this group six months later. They see John has become successful. His bonus checks are sky-rocketing. His lifestyle and attitude are completely changed. They know you can build leaders and make them successful.

What's their natural tendency? To yell, "Me next! Me next! I'm ready to become an MLM leader! Please, please let me be the one you choose to build as leader #2!"

Your searching for motivated raw leadership is over. Once you do the job right, the waiting line is always full. Sure beats standing in the middle of the street begging bystanders to join your MLM program.

Great MLM potential talent will come to you if you do your job right. All you have to do is pick the next motivated distributor to enter your six-month training program.

Hey! Do you hear that dull thud in the background? That's your competition falling down from exhaustion. They can't keep up with your pace. They are still doing it the hard way.

If they chose to steal someone else's MLM leaders, they are now wondering why their competitors stole these same leaders. There is no loyalty among thieves.

Compare that with the loyalty from your MLM leaders. You are best friends, partners, co-workers and, you have invested six months as mentor to take your distributor from rags to riches. Is your new leader going to jump ship to a sleazy sponsor who doesn't want to help him, but only wants to cash in on his efforts? Your new leader appreciates what you have done to change his life. There is security in your MLM leader investment.

And, if your competition spent the last six months sponsoring distributors, your competition will spend the next six months looking for replacements. These tail-chasers are easy to identify. They have been in MLM for years. They don't have a single downline leader and have to struggle to make minimum wage. If they had to do their career over, surely they would have been miles ahead to build a leader a year.

For stable, consistent, fabulous bonus checks, invest in MLM leaders. Oh yeah, also wear earplugs. The dull thuds of your defeated competition hitting the ground can be deafening.

The $93,000 Recruiting System

Who has the best MLM sales presentation?

Who can give professional presentations in his sleep?

Who can answer all the prospects' questions?

The old pro, Mr. MLM. He's the man with the experience who has seen it all. He has mastered every presentation technique. Plus, Mr. MLM is surrounded by his experienced team of leaders. Just call him the *answer man*.

Now, why is it that the new, inexperienced MLM distributor can sponsor circles around the old pro?

It appears to be a mystery. We all have seen it. The brand new, wet-behind-the-ears, greenhorn distributor goes out of the opportunity meeting full of enthusiasm and signs up 10 or 20 new distributors. During the same time period, the old pro, Mr. MLM sponsors no one. Mr. MLM has the skills and experience, but the new enthusiastic recruit brings in more new distributors.

The answers to this mystery are belief and momentum.

Belief

The old pro has been around the block. He sees some distributors make it, but many more fail. He knows everyone won't make the money he or she desires, and his belief shows through in his presentation.

The new recruit knows this is the greatest opportunity available to mankind. His burning, missionary enthusiasm overcomes his lack of sales skills, presentation skills, and knowledge. The new recruit has *leadership charisma.*

Who do people wish to follow?

Will they follow the rocket scientists with all the answers, or follow the charismatic, enthusiastic leaders with less knowledge but a vision for the future? We've never elected rocket scientists to the presidency but we've elected an actor with considerably less mental power. Enough said?

Momentum

We all know the illustration of what happens to a penny that is doubled every day. After one month, you're rich. How many people do you know who have doubled a penny every day for a month? None? Why?

In real life, there is a deceleration of momentum with time. In other words, the momentum gets slower and slower everyday. If bacteria doubled every few hours, in a matter of weeks the world would be just one big germ hotel. If each Amway distributor who joined in 1959 would double his group every week, everyone in China, Russia, and India would be selling laundry detergent to each other.

The point is: The longer an organization exists, the slower its growth. The old pro's group is at the end of the momentum cycle. Hopefully, there are enough new recruits to offset the dropouts.

The new recruit is at the beginning of the momentum cycle. Everyone is jumping on his bandwagon. The jumping is contagious and each new prospect catches the fever.

So, how can we utilize the two keys of the **$93,000 Recruiting System,** *momentum* and *belief,* to build our downline fast?

Step one is to review the *Stair Step Solution* recruiting technique in *Big Al's How To Create A Recruiting Explosion.* This is the surest way to create *momentum.* While you sponsor your way down through your new recruit's downline, the fear of loss principle forces fast sign-ups. Also, the *Stair Step* recruiting technique builds multiple levels of *locked-in* loyalty to reduce dropouts and distributor turnover. The *Stair Step* recruiting technique is truly one of the most powerful tools in building profitable downlines.

But how do we add the extra dimension and belief to create the **$93,000 Recruiting System?**

New recruits can produce recruiting miracles if they *believe* they cannot fail. And we as leaders can provide that needed *belief* with a simple, unselfish, all-out commitment. Here is how we sell the new recruit on his guaranteed success. We say:

"John, how would you like me, your sponsor, as your full-time employee? That's right. I'm willing to work for you exclusively to build you an organization fast. I'll make *two-on-one* presentations anytime, day or night. I'll spend my available time training your new recruits and helping them with presentations and meetings. I'll even find new prospects whom I'll recruit into your downline. In other words, if you want to make a commitment for success, I'll work for you full-time until you get there."

What is your new recruit going to say? What does your new recruit feel inside? He has the *belief* that his success is guaranteed. How could he possibly fail with your experienced, upline assistance? He knows you will assist him until he succeeds. Now watch his enthusiasm and his group grow.

As a leader, you can make your new recruit's belief even stronger by getting *additional* assistance from your upline leaders. For instance, after getting your new recruit excited about your full-time commitment, add fuel to the fire by saying:

"And that's not all. My sponsor has committed two full days a week to work with your downline. He is a meeting expert and also specializes in getting referrals. That means even more new distributors in your group. In addition, his sponsor committed $300 to your advertising program and promised to personally sign up two new distributors in your group. Between my working full-time, my sponsor working two days a week, and my sponsor's sponsor helping too, don't you think we'll blow the lid off this town?"

Now, do you think your new recruit feels commitment and truly *believes* in his ultimate success? Nothing motivates better than *helping people reach their goals*.

Finally, how do we translate this system into **$93,000** or more?

Consider this. Most leaders spread their efforts too thin. They try to reach levels of achievement and ranks too fast. This leaves them with turnover and the time-wasting efforts of rebuilding decimated groups.

For instance, let's imagine that your goal was to build four first-level distributors to the rank of *Big Time Leader*.

A Big Time Leader position required 20 distributors in the downline plus $2,000 in product volume. Many leaders would sponsor four distributors and work with all four simultaneously. At the end of one year, maybe all four first-level distributors would make it to the Leader level, but at least two or three of them would have weak groups.

Compare that method with the following:

What if you sponsored just one first-level distributor and said, "If you want to be a Leader, I'm willing to be your full-time employee for at least one month, or until you reach the Leader level. You'll have my full-time support to help you make presentations. Any leads or prospects I run across will go into your downline, etc., etc. Plus, my sponsor has committed etc., etc. Plus my sponsor's sponsor has committed etc., etc."

Do you think that with your help, plus your sponsor's help, and your sponsor's sponsor help, you could make your committed new recruit reach the level of *Big Time Leader* within 30 days?

Of course!

Maybe your new recruit would reach the *Big Time Leader* level in as little as one week!

What does this mean for your organization? You could build a brand new first level *Big Time Leader* group every 30 days! After one year, you would have 12 solid first level groups.

Now that's The **$93,000 Recruiting System.***

***Disclaimer:** The above method requires work. Lazy, slothful, negative distributors are not advised to try this without professional upline assistance.

Life in MLM
is almost perfect

At least one bad event will happen to your multilevel company this year. It's no big deal. No company can go on forever with lucky events followed by good fortune followed by miracle good news. While we want our MLM company to have good fortune forever, occasionally someone steps on part of our dreams.

For example, maybe your MLM company backorders or discontinues your group's favorite product. Maybe a local trash tabloid reports that your company's president is secretly a two-headed alien who performs secret animal sacrifices. Or, disgruntled downline distributors form their own clone MLM company and try to steal your leaders. Or, out of thousands of product orders, your MLM company made a mistake on someone's order (shudder, stress, check our wills, sound the panic alert!).

What happens when your MLM company has the occasional but predictable problems? Do you lose your leaders? Do you spend hours on the phone trying to salvage your downline? Do you apologize, sympathize, and worry into the night?

No. You prepare yourself in advance for problems. Your MLM company will have problems, your upline will have problems, your downline will have problems, and that's just how life is. If you don't believe that problems will ever happen to your MLM business, that illusion will pass shortly.

How do you prepare your leaders for bad news, backorders, fulfillment mistakes, hurt feelings, phone calls mixed up or not returned, etc.? Simple. Tell them the truth in advance.

You might say: "John, before you make a total commitment to building your downline, you need to know the facts. First, our MLM company is not perfect. There will be some problems in the future. Worst yet, our MLM company employs humans, and you know how they can make mistakes. The good news is that our MLM company tries its best to fix mistakes when they happen. Now, knowing that it won't be 100% uninterrupted smooth sailing in the future, are you still willing to make a total commitment to build your MLM downline?"

Normally, John will answer, "No problem. I understand there will be ups and downs. Thanks for being honest with me. There are problems in every job and business, so I know better than to try to look for perfection."

Now, when the inevitable problems do occur, you've prepared your leaders for a little pep talk. Let's say that the problem of the month was . . . The company changed its labels from light green to dark green. Oooo-hhhh. Now your downline is really worried. Your leaders are thinking of switching to another company that offers labels in a very light green. They swear they never want to live through another label color change. Their customers complain. Their distributors feel confused. This problem is now a major mess and threatens the productivity and retention of your downline.

But, you had the foresight to prepare your downline for eventual challenges (sounds better than life-threatening problems). Here's your pep talk:

"John, remember when you first made the commitment to build your MLM downline? We discussed that problems would be in our future and would give us a few stumbling blocks along the way. Well, this label color change is one of those problems. It looks like a big deal now, but if we compare it to a ten- or twenty-year career, it's just one of those problems that's going to happen. Sometimes we leap forward, sometimes we take a step or two back, but overall, we leaders focus on long-term, steady progress.

"That's what makes us different from the average MLM distributor who has one bad experience and quits. Then, the average distributor has to go out and invest and build a brand new group with a new company. That's a lot of time and money invested in training and building a new business. There's no income coming in, just expenses during these transition periods. And just when the average distributor gets to profit in his new MLM company, B-A-N-G! Another problem pops up. I guess that sums up the difference between average MLM distributors and leaders like us, John. They never make any money because they don't have our long-term vision.

"I bet if their mother served one bad meal, they would never visit her again. If their bank made a mistake on their checking account, they'd give up using money. I sure hope you and I can get through to most of your downline that this is just one of those problems along the way. Sure hope that they'll have the good business sense we do to see the big picture."

Will your pep talk work? Not always. But it's better than no pep talk at all. And, your pep talks always work better when you prepare your leaders early in their career that no company is perfect and that they should expect problems along the way.

Will you save the distributors in your leader's downline? Not all of them. Many new MLM distributors believe that success comes from signing an application in a hot new company that will never have any problems. They don't believe that MLM success requires work, effort, patience and long-term commitment. It kind of makes you sick to listen to a new MLM distributor say: "I'm not having anything to do with MLM. I worked hard for two weeks with a multilevel opportunity, and then they had problems. That just ruined any chance I had for success." I wonder if his job only requires two weeks of effort and then he can retire for life?

So, if a distributor is looking for an excuse not to work — then any excuse will do.

I've never seen a plaque that read:

All The World Loves A Quitter

Hype from the top

Ever wonder what prospects think during our opportunity meetings? How does the word *skeptical* sound? Why? Because leaders become so excited about their MLM opportunity, that hype sneaks into even professional presentations. Now, hype isn't bad — in small dosages. You wouldn't want a monologue from a lobotomized accountant for your opportunity presentation. Excitement is important to get complacent guests to decide now. But, excitement that comes only from hype breeds skepticism.

How does over-hype presented by the speaker at an opportunity meeting sound? Something like this.

"In the next ten years, 50% of all products sold will be sold via multilevel marketing. It's the marketing wave of the future."

The guests begin to think.

"Hmmm. Let's see now. I just read where 81% of sales occurs at retail outlets and 18% of sales is done through telemarketing. Boy, I really hate those automatic telephone dialers. My brother-in-law says 37% of sales occurs through direct mail. Seems fair to me. Just look at all those catalogs I get in the mail.

Only 8% of sales are through door-to-door sales. Home Shopping Network does 10% of sales. And now with 50% of sales by multi-level marketing, . . . gee, that totals 204%! I'd better go home and do some thinking about this."

The MLM leader giving the opportunity looks over his audience and sees the guests silently nodding. The MLM leader thinks:

"Yeah, they're right in the palm of my hand. Look at them nod and agree. Just like sheep. Maybe I should have told them 110% of all products sold would be through multilevel marketing. I bet that would really excite them."

The guests in the audience think:

"If he exaggerates this, he probably exaggerates everything in his presentation. Better think it over at home over a couple of beers. Boy, a couple of beers sure sound good."

The end of the opportunity meeting is predictable. The leader pressures the guests to join now. The guests reply,

"I'll have to go home and think it over."

Simple courtesy, truth, and respect for our prospects' intelligence prevent hype. Prospects will stay around after opportunity meetings and get involved in MLM if they don't feel the leader and the opportunity are phony.

Q. What do MLM Junkies call an opportunity meeting where the guests are up to their necks in hype?

A. Not enough hype.

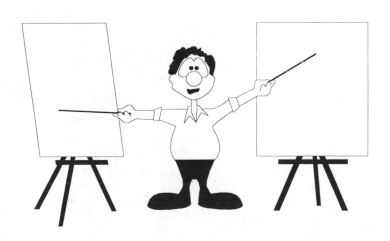

Chain letters have value

Chain letters aren't all bad. They're not really that good either.

However, chain letters can help build your business. How? Certainly not by participating. The secret is that you get the names and addresses of brand new people who want to earn extra money.

Who participates in chain letters? Usually novices, people getting started in mail order. Experienced mail order business people and MLMers know better than to throw away their money on chain letters. The meager chain letter profits go to the original promoter and the mailing list companies. Of course, the Post Office does pretty good on its stamp sales too.

What is unique about chain letter participants? They all sincerely want to make money. They invested their own money into printing and postage, and they made a genuine effort by mailing their letters. Sounds like a pretty good prospect.

What else do we know about this prospect? First, they will lose money on their chain letter participation. They may become discouraged about extra income, or they might look for other opportunities to reach their dreams.

Second, the chain letter participants will receive a flood of "me too" offers and solicitations to join opportunities as others see their name and address in the mail.

How can you separate your offering and turn this hot prospect with the right idea (make extra money) and the wrong vehicle (chain letters) into an MLM leader for your downline?

By going the extra mile. Your competition sees the name and address of the chain letter participant. Quickly, they photocopy a company brochure and application and drop it in the mail with a short note saying, "Try this. It's really hot." This doesn't impress the chain letter participant. He gets 10 or 20 new offers like this every day in his mail. He knows he is just another name and address to you.

What do successful recruiters do? They write a letter. It could be handwritten, or even typed — but personal. They ask the prospect, "How is it going? Wanted to strike up some correspondence with you. We have similar interests, making money. Drop me a line when you get a chance."

The prospect sees a personal letter from someone who cares. Some prospects will write back, offer their phone number, or call you direct. Personal letters are hard to ignore, especially if they are sincere and handwritten.

Now, on the second correspondence, you might mention your program and your experiences. Once you have your foot in the door, you can become a mentor to your new prospect. The secret is to get your foot in the door.

You don't need overwhelming numbers of personally recruited distributors to be successful. You only need a couple of good leaders to make a fantastic income in MLM. So why not invest your time in building these raw recruits into highly skilled MLMers?

You may have to sort through a lot of not interested, lazy, get-rich-quick scam artists, etc. to find a few sincere prospects. But, you only need a couple of good leaders to make your career a success.

One enhancement on this technique is the direct phone call. One distributor recruited 12 new distributors in one month. How? She looked up phone numbers of chain letter participants and called them directly. Many are listed in their local phone directories. More amazing is that this was the first phone call the chain letter participants ever received. No one else made the effort to call long-distance directory assistance or to research out- of-town directories at the local library. The phone call really set this distributor apart from her competition's second-generation photo-copied brochures. Phone calls are very, very personal.

What is the essence of this technique?

Personal, sincere interest in the prospect.

If you rented a mailing list of chain letter participants and bulk-mailed a few thousand photocopied letters, you'd say that chain letter participants are useless. Your response would be dismal.

The secret is a short, handwritten or very personalized typewritten letter that motivates the prospect to reply. Now, you have a friend. And wouldn't you like to have a friend who sincerely wants to make money as your prospect?

News Update: Edward Green (the original king of chain letters) recently announced a new, streamlined version of the chain letter where all the participants' money is sent directly to him, bypassing those greedy middlemen of the Post Office, printers, and list brokers.

Streamline your business

Who takes up most of your time?

Group 1: The self-starters, the leaders, the hard-working MLMers who are actively building their business?

Or,

Group 2: The whiners, complainers, the unmotivated prospects looking for a freebie handout?

Group 2 wins easily. These are the people who sign up after you loan them the sign-up kit money. They call you daily asking:

A) Have you built my downline yet?

B) How much bonus should I expect this month?

C) Why do you expect me to make contacts or presentations?

D) Why are the company's products so expensive?

E) Why doesn't the company advertise for me?

F) Why doesn't the company take the retail orders for me?

G) Why doesn't the company advance my bonus checks to get started?

H) Why aren't the bonus checks sent directly to the bank so I won't have to make a trip?

I) Why doesn't the company give away products as samples to get customers?

"THREE THINGS ARE CERTAIN IN LIFE... DEATH, TAXES AND MONDAYS."

J) Why doesn't the company pay people to try the product and just send us bonus checks to keep out of the way?

K) Why do I have to go to opportunity meetings? I already know how they end.

L) When can I retire? You told me it would be fast and easy at the opportunity meeting.

M) Why should I buy products? There should have been some free products in the sign-up kit you bought for me.

And the list goes on.

As MLM leaders, we hear these requests daily from recruits who want to work their MLM business for a couple of weeks and then retire with a guaranteed monthly fortune.

These dreamers and complainers take up to 80% of an MLM leader's time.

How do you solve this problem? Simply write down the names and phone numbers of your dreaming, complaining freeloaders and give them to the competition. Tell your competitor that these are MLMers looking for a change of program (well, they are MLMers and they would be willing to consider something better). You can be assured that your competition will promise them a much better opportunity than you have provided.

The bottom-line? The freeloaders will keep your competition busy while you are out looking for leaders.

Ad in a "Personals" column:

Lazy, SWM, MLM junkie looking for SWF with established downline for marriage and financial support.

How to get all the prospects you want

". . . and that's why I think this MLM opportunity is not only the opportunity of the decade — but it's the opportunity of the century!"

You have just finished giving your finest presentation to your prospect. You covered every sales point and possible objection. Now is the moment of truth.

Your prospect replies:

"No! No! No! A thousand times NO! You make me sick! You are disgusting! You are a disgrace to the human race! You are using up valuable oxygen on the Earth. Get off this planet and out of this universe! I never want to see you again as long as I live!"

Now, many distributors would consider this as a "no."

While this may not be your hottest prospect, all is not lost.

How can you salvage something from this bad situation?

You can ask for referrals. If your present prospect is undecided (or outright hostile and negative), he may know other people who would welcome your offer. You might try saying something like this:

"I can appreciate you may not be interested in my MLM opportunity today, but I tell you what. Why don't you give me the names of three people who want to earn a bit of extra money — and I promise never to bother you again for as long as I live. Fair enough?"

Chances are that your prospect might give you a couple referrals to get rid of you. Will you always get referrals? No. But if you never ask for referrals, you are guaranteed zero referrals. When you ask, at least you have a chance.

So, how can you ask for referrals in a way that will produce the best results?

Why not take a lesson from the world's premier referral gatherer, the insurance salesman? Have you ever had an insurance salesman in your home? How did he ask for referrals? When you decided not to buy his insurance did he say:

"Well, if you're not going to buy this insurance, who else do you know that I can peddle this stuff to?"

Of course not. If he did ask for referrals this way, you might have replied by saying:

"Gee, I really don't know anybody who needs insurance. I'm an orphan with no relatives. And before that I was a hermit in the Himalayan Mountains. I just moved to this town 20 years ago and don't know a soul. My Christmas list was lost in the fire . . . etc."

You would give excuses, not referrals.

So how does the life insurance salesman get you to jog your memory for hot prospects? Instead of asking who needs insurance, the insurance salesman asks for specific situations in a more tactful manner. He'll say:

"I understand that you don't feel a need for insurance today, but could you do me a favor?"

"Who do you know just got promoted in his job?"

"Who recently had a baby?"

"Who do you know really loves his family?"

"Who do you know just bought a house?"

"Who do you know has his own business?"

"Who do you know wants financial security?"

This line of questioning produces better results. You can think of people in each of these specific situations, and your insurance salesman is looking forward to sales presentations with them all.

How can you apply this technique to your MLM business?

When your prospect turns your opportunity down, don't say:

"Well, who else do you know that I can get into this pyramid scheme deal?"

If you do, your prospect will reply:

"Gee, I really don't know anybody who needs extra money or your opportunity. I'm an orphan with no relatives. And before that I was a hermit in the Himalayan Mountains. I just moved to this town 20 years ago and don't know a soul. My Christmas list was lost in the fire . . . etc."

Instead, try asking your prospect these questions:

"Who do you know would like to earn some extra money?"

"Who hates his job?"

"Who hates his boss?"

"Who do you know would like to have a part-time income while still keeping his present job?"

"Who would like to move from an apartment to a home?"

"Who do you know who enjoys traveling?"

"Who wants to save up for college?"

"Do any of your friends want to own their own business?"

Now your prospects can give you names of people they know fit these situations. Will you get presentation appointments with them all? No, but you will get enough appointments to keep you busy and you'll never have to cold-call for prospects again.

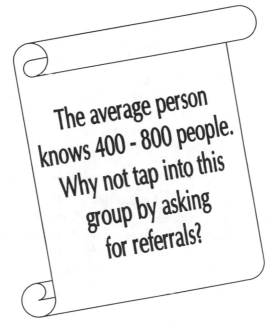

The average person knows 400 - 800 people. Why not tap into this group by asking for referrals?

MLM mail order tips

It happens to everybody. You get into multilevel and you start thinking big, real big. Why bother with working hard, doing single presentations, bringing guests to opportunity meetings, and taking time to train new distributors? That's too low-tech. Why not use the power of the U.S. Postal Service to recruit thousands of new distributors through mail order recruiting? It's fast, easy, there's no rejection, simple, and oh yes, very, very, very expensive.

Mail order multilevel recruiting appears to be the "get rich, real quick" method to multilevel success. It sounds so good. Just relax at home, lick a few stamps while watching TV, and wait for the applications to come flowing into your mailbox. This is the ultimate shortcut to multilevel disaster.

What usually happens?

First, the starry-eyed distributor purchases some very expensive literature from the home office. If you're going to mail for recruits, you might as well impress them with the finest four-color literature money can buy.

Second, the new distributor, who hasn't written a letter since high school, writes the perfect motivational cover letter that will certainly outperform anything an expensive copywriter could produce. (Actually, an honest, from-the-heart letter really does work, but it's the typos and misspellings that usually kill the amateur effort.)

Third, the new distributor designs a few pieces of literature, charts, business strategies, etc. to include in his customized mail package. Why not impress the prospects with volumes of documentation? The local quick-print shop will make his overhead from the few thousand pieces ordered for this fantastic mail campaign.

Fourth, all the relatives are invited over to the house for pizza. Only when they arrive do they find out it's really a fold-and-stuff-the-envelope party. After a few hours licking envelopes, they won't feel like eating much pizza. At least this will keep unwanted relatives from dropping by over the next year.

Fifth, there's the required bank loan for the postage. If it weren't for chain letters and multilevel mail order recruiting efforts, the postal deficit would double. I guess mail order recruiting is kind of a patriotic act after all.

Finally, you wait and watch TV reruns for the next several weeks, hoping for a return on your investment. And it doesn't come.

What do you receive? Address corrections from that "guaranteed wonderful" mailing list you bought, solicitations from other multilevel mail order recruiters, and the first installment notice on your bank loan. On the bright side, you get one application from a prospect in the small town of Nowhere, Far-Away, Romania. He wants you to travel 1,500 miles to train him and show him how to get started in this multilevel thing. Airfare is only a few hundred bucks each way, so hey, "This mail order thing could really pay off, eh?"

Because of high costs, low returns, and bad experiences, most MLMers try mail order recruiting just one time and then get sour on the whole concept of MLM.

But despite overwhelming odds, multilevelers will continue to mail for new distributors. Is it a genetic deficiency? An evil message secretly recorded on subliminal tapes? Or can it be our, "We'll-try-anything-to-be-successful," spirit? For whatever the reason, the mailings will go on, and on, and on.

So, if the mailings must go on, what can we do to minimize the waste and maximize the returns? Here are three tips you can use starting now.

Get A Mentor

Your mailing will arrive in the same mailbox, at the same time, as the expensive mailing packages produced by Madison Avenue. Let's face it. You're going to be in direct competition with some billion-dollar financed professionals. To compete, you must get all the information and education you can. A trip to the local library, or the outright purchase of a couple of mail order books would be nice, but nothing substitutes for experience. Find a pro who is successfully mailing for multilevel recruits. In one hour he can give you a year's worth of book learning. He can share the techniques he uses to squash the competition, to stand out from the crowd, and to target his mailings to keep his overall costs manageable. If you can't find a pro to share his success techniques with you, be prepared to join the mail order crowd that finances the postal union.

Looking Good

If your literature and cover letter look like a fourth-generation chain letter, it deserves to be treated like one — in the wastebasket. Don't bother investing postage and labor to mail wastebasket stuffing via first class. America's landfills are filling up. Nobody will believe in your million-dollar opportunity if it's printed on a fuzzy photocopy from your often-repaired office copier. At the very least, get a good quick printer to make a clear copy of your offer.

Mailing Frugally

Don't spend much money on the initial mailer. Use something inexpensive and simple on your initial contact. Then, if your prospect shows interest, you can invest your dollars in mailing a first-class package to a qualified, interested, hot prospect.

Let's say you mailed a $2 printed package to 1,000 prospects. Total printing investment: $2,000. With a 1% return, you'd have 10 hot prospects with a $2 literature package in their hands. So, for $2,000 investment you have 10 hot prospects.

You spent $200 on each prospect just to get $2 worth of literature into their hands! Ouch!

For the same $200 you could bribe a stranger on the street to pretend he's interested in your material.

Now, consider the difference if you mailed a 25¢ printed package to 1,000 prospects. Total printing investment: $250. That's an initial savings of $1,750. At a 1% return, you would again have 10 hot prospects, but you would only have $25 invested in each prospect.

Using the same $2,000 budget, here's the difference. Now, you can afford to send a deluxe follow-up printed package worth $175 each to each of your 10 prospects. What kind of impression could you make with a $175 printed package? A big impression.

The point is:

Mail inexpensively for leads, then invest your printing dollars in follow-up packages to these leads.

Zero Sum Theory

How does betting at the racetrack work? Does the racetrack create money to pay the winners? Or does the racetrack take money from the losers to pay the winners?

Obviously, the winners win at the expense of the losers. No money is created at the racetrack. There are no printing presses churning out dollars in the stables.

The winners collect from the money wagered by all the bettors. Therefore, it follows that the winners can never collect more than the total amount wagered. The racetrack cannot convert a one-dollar bill into $1.15.

If everyone went to the racetrack and bet one dollar, and every bettor received $1.15, we would have to rewrite the theory of mathematics or question the business proficiency of the racetrack.

How Do Racetracks Really Work?

You go to the betting window and wager one dollar (for illustration purposes only. Minimum wager is normally $3.00). The racetrack keeps 10 cents for overhead and profit and places 90 cents into the payoff pool to be shared by the winning tickets. This means that the winners can only receive 90% of the total amount wagered.

Let's imagine that the bettors wagered $1,000 on the first race. The racetrack takes $100 (10%) for overhead and profit, and disburses $900 to the winning bettors.

On the second race, the bettors only have $900 remaining from their original $1,000 investment. When they wager the remaining $900, the racetrack takes $90 (10%) for overhead and profit. The winning bettors on the second race receive $810 from the payoff pool.

On the third race, the bettors only have $810 remaining from their original $1,000 investment. When they wager the remaining $810, the racetrack takes $81 (10%) for overhead and profit. The winning bettors on the third race receive $729 from the payoff pool.

On the fourth race, the bettors only have $729 remaining from their original $1,000 investment. When they wager the remaining $729, the racetrack takes $73 (10%) for overhead and profit. The winning bettors on the fourth race receive $656 from the payoff pool.

On the fifth race, the bettors only have $656 remaining from their original $1,000 investment. When they wager the remaining $656, the racetrack takes $66 (10%) for overhead and profit. The winning bettors on the fourth race receive $590 from the payoff pool.

By the time the eighth race has ended, there is only $430 remaining for the payoff pool. In other words, the original amount wagered has been reduced 57%. The racetrack doesn't create money; it only takes money.

If the betting public is guaranteed to lose money at the racetrack, why do they come?

People enjoy the entertainment. Also, there is the remote possibility of being one of the few winners at the expense of the losing bettors. So, for most of those attending, they consider their guaranteed losses as payment for entertainment. They are getting entertainment value for their money.

The Lottery

Does the government print money to pay off lottery winners? Or, does the government take money from the losing ticket purchasers to pay the winners?

Again, the government pays the winners from the proceeds of the lottery ticket sales.

How The Lottery Works

The government keeps 50% of the lottery ticket sales for overhead and their general revenue fund. The other 50% of the lottery ticket sales is placed in the payoff pool to be shared by the winning ticket holders. Does the government do well with this arrangement? You bet!

Does this mean that people who buy lottery tickets are guaranteed to lose 50% of their investment? Yes, but they receive a little excitement and entertainment for their $1 ticket. It's a small amount so people don't mind.

In both the racetrack and the lottery examples, people are guaranteed to lose part of their original investment. However, they feel they are getting value (entertainment) in return.

How Multilevel Companies Work

Multilevel companies generally have the following disbursement for money received from distributors:

    50% Bonuses

    25% Cost of Product/Service

    25% Overhead and Profit

This means that for each dollar spent by multilevel distributors, only 50 cents will return to the field as bonuses.

Like lotteries and racetracks, multilevel companies do not print their own money. They can only disburse a portion of the monies they receive back to the distributor force. The balance is used for product value, profit, and overhead.

Will multilevel distributors participate in multilevel companies knowing that they will lose 50% of their investment? Yes, as long as the multilevel company provides value for their money.

If the multilevel company had no product or service, or a product or service of negligible value, distributors would quickly tire of losing 50% of their money.

Here is the mistake that permeates many leaders' downlines. Too many of their distributors join just for the money and forget about product value. They have the misconception that everybody can make more money than they invest. It's mathematically impossible!

These distributors recruit others by saying they will receive bonus checks larger than their investment. It can't happen! Only a few distributors can receive bonus checks larger than their investment. Most distributors will receive smaller or no bonus checks at all.

Multilevel companies cannot receive one dollar in revenue, provide a product or service, pay overhead, make a profit, and still pay our $1.15 in bonuses. It's a fact that most distributors will receive no bonus checks.

This misconception leads distributors to say the following to new recruits:

"Don't worry about the product. Even if you don't need it or think it's too expensive, the important thing is that you need only three distributors to break even. When you get your fourth distributor, you're in the profit!"

The new recruits join a program and recruit a few distributors. Their new distributors don't make enough in bonuses to cover their monthly investment, so they drop out. Now the original distributor's bonus check drops below his monthly investment, so he drops out. His sponsor's bonus check drops below his original investment, so his sponsor drops out.

When a distributor uses the power of the marketing plan only to recruit another distributor, he is doomed to fail. No marketing plan can make everyone a winner by providing them with bonus checks larger than their original investment.

When you say it only takes three people for you to break even, you are really saying:

"Three people must lose their investment for you to break even."

If we put it this way, we see why using the marketing plan only to convince prospects to join is doomed to fail. How long are distributors on the bottom going to lose money so their sponsors can break even?

The Solution

All multilevel programs that fail are based solely on the marketing plan. They offer little or no product/service value for the distributor's investment. For example, they market a bottle of vitamins for $60 that costs only $10 in a store, or an expensive travel or discount service that could normally be obtained free. If the product or service is not a good deal for the distributor on the bottom, he'll drop out. Then his sponsor is on the bottom, and he'll drop out, etc.

The product/service value must stand on its own. There will always be distributors on the bottom, so they will have to purchase the product/service on its own merits, without the benefit of a bonus rebate.

The secret for long downline life is the actual product/service value. You must decide if the product or service a multilevel company provides is:

#1. Fairly priced.

#2. Wanted by the public.

You will need many distributors in your downline who will join your program just for the product/service. These distributors are the bonus foundation for the leaders who need the larger bonuses to promote your program. If your leaders are constantly replacing their new distributors, they are running in circles and will find some place else to run.

Leaders can only con, promise, and hype distributors for so long. People aren't dumb. They know when they are getting a bad deal. So make sure your program offers the distributors on the bottom a good deal.

Don't get caught in trap of pleading, calling and begging your downline to stay in a program that isn't providing value. It's a losing battle. Make sure your program has value so you never have to be ashamed of introducing a distributor to your program.

No more boring meetings, no more product deliveries. Joe was on the shortcut to wealth.

Shortcut #1
Why wait for one's name to move to the top? A few creative changes can put you ahead of the crowd.

Send $5 to:
1. Distributor Joe, Route 1, B
2. Joe & Associates, P.O. Box
3. Joe's Entrepreneur Opportun
4. D.J. World Enterprises, P
5. D.Joe Marketing, RT.1,

But a disgruntled postman, forced to work by carrying Joe's extra mail, senses something is wrong.

In the bowels of the central Post Office, the local postmaster scientifically investigates one of Joe's letters.

All right boys. Go get him!

A secret meeting at Postal Command considers Joe's chain letter threat to the national security.

The Postal Service pays a visit to Joe to discuss his recent mailing.

Joe is consoled by his crack attorney.

Got to go. My manicure appointment is in 10 minutes. Maybe we can plea bargain for the death penalty.

Justice was swift. Joe receives a cruel and unusual sentence worse than the death penalty.

KANGAROO COURT

Guilty! Guilty! Guilty! I sentence Joe Distributor to work one week as a postal employee.

Joe diligently serves his one-week sentence as a highly paid postal worker. The sun was awful.

Hey buddy! Here's the pizza and beer you ordered.

But the one-week sentence had serious side effects. Joe gained 10 lbs.!

Master Hustler, Sleaze Shallowman sees profit in Joe's dilemma.

Sleaze "Humanitarian" Shallowman offered Joe numerous MLM opportunities.

Joe was impressed with Sleaze's courage. Who said sponsors don't care about their downlines?

ARRRGH!!

Gee. What a mess I'm in. I wonder what else could go wrong?

Little did Distributor Joe know that the worst was yet to come.

KILL!

The MasterCard Collection Agency comes to Joe's front door.

Joe uses his superior negotiating skills to put off his aggressive creditors.

Pssst. Hey Big Al. Could you meet me at the house tomorrow? I sorta have a problem.

So Joe, you met Sleaze "The Greed" Shallowman, eh?

Mailing for leaders

Do you live in New York City? Probably not. But for the moment, imagine you live in the *Big Apple*. Are you ready to start mailing to the hottest list of qualified prospects to build your downline organization?

Let's get started.

You've picked the right list. You have the hottest multilevel opportunity known to mankind. You've written the perfect motivating sales letter. You offer the finest in upline support. So let the letters flow.

Your first response comes from Butte's Bluff, Montana. His letter reads:

Wow! Sounds like a terrific multilevel opportunity. Your upline support system sounds impressive.

Very few multilevel leaders offer to give meetings and training anywhere, anytime. So, here's my application. My first meeting will be in the Badger Lodge next Wednesday night. Since I'm brand new to multilevel, could you please bring some extra training tools with you when you come to give the meeting? I'm not sure how many sets you should bring as it will be hard to predict how many guests will be there. I really don't know anybody personally to invite, so I ran a one-minute ad on our local radio station. Who knows? Maybe the lodge will be overflowing with prospects. I don't have a phone yet, so it's impossible to call me with your plane reservations. I'll just assume you'll be on the 6:40 a.m. bush pilot special on Wednesday morning. I'll meet you there. My pickup is broken, but it is only a short walk over the mountain to town. That'll give us time to talk.

See you there!

Homer Beaner

Ouch! This really hurts. Yes, you did promise upline support. However, the round trip flight is $973 plus lodging. Plus, how many people will be at the Badger Lodge? Historically, a one-minute radio ad will pull zero response. Should you invest $973 plus lodging for the privilege of hiking over the mountain with Homer? Gee, you can't even contact him and give him pointers to run his own meeting. Do you abandon your enthusiastic recruit? Break your word of honor? Get a job at 7-Eleven?

An ounce of prevention is worth at least $973. Many years ago a famous MLM mailing expert explained his inside secret to success. He said:

"Mail only for leaders. You can't efficiently train and support distributors. Leaders can give their own meetings, train their people, and be productive without your presence. All they ask for is your coaching. So, don't tailor your recruiting letter to distributors. Focus your offer on leaders."

Well, it doesn't take a rocket scientist to see this makes sense. To train and nurture a new distributor in Butte's Bluff, Montana could entail several trips a year. For the same investment in time and money, you could effectively coach and help several MLM leaders build their businesses. Hopefully, you could eventually train enough MLM leaders nationwide that a new distributor in Butte's Bluff, Montana would have a full-time MLM leader in his back yard. You can perform a more beneficial service to new recruits by networking them with a local leader. Phone calls are nice, but local support and training are what new recruits desire and deserve.

So, when making a multilevel recruiting offer by mail, why not try the following headlines:

Are you a successful MLM leader?
Then please read on.
~ ~ ~ ~ ~ ~ ~ ~

Do you have MLM experience?
Let's talk.
~ ~ ~ ~ ~ ~ ~ ~

For MLM pros only.
~ ~ ~ ~ ~ ~ ~ ~

Only leaders please.
~ ~ ~ ~ ~ ~ ~ ~

Are you self-motivated?
~ ~ ~ ~ ~ ~ ~ ~

Can you execute our
proven success plan?

While your response may be less, your quality will be better. And, you will be corresponding with people you can really help.

What happens if you continue to mail recruiting offers with these headlines?

Super opportunity for riches!
~ ~ ~ ~ ~ ~ ~ ~

Anybody can do this business!
~ ~ ~ ~ ~ ~ ~ ~

Get rich now with our super MLM program!
~ ~ ~ ~ ~ ~ ~ ~

I can make you rich! Call now!

Well, pack your bags and get ready to see America. Not only will you drain your bank account, but you will only be giving lip-service to many new MLM distributors who need and deserve full-time local support to become a MLM leader.

To make matters worse, there are plenty of mailing myths that can cost MLM leaders time and money. Let's look at a few now.

Myth #1
Avoid a dirty list

Nixies. The most dreaded word in any mailer's vocabulary. What is a nixie? You spent your precious postage to mail your offer to John Doe. A few weeks later your letter is returned to you unopened. The Postal Service has stamped the envelope: "Return To Sender, Address Unknown" (sounds like a hit song), "Moved, Left No Forwarding Address," "Moved, Forwarding Time Expired" or some other way of saying:

"Here's your letter back. Thanks for your postage donation to our retirement fund."

That's what a nixie is. Wasted postage.

So, conventional wisdom says, "Avoid a dirty list. Nixies are bad. Only rent clean, current updated mailing lists."

Are nixies bad? Let's look at how nixies are made.

Every year people move. Some estimate that up to 18% or 20% move every year! If one out of five Americans move every year, even a current mailing list will have some nixies. That translates to 18% a year. That means each month 1.5% of the population move. Let's see how fast nixies can creep into your list.

For example, on January 1 you mail 1,000 offers. On February 1, only 985 will still be at their current address as 15 (1.5%) have moved. On March 1, only 970 will still be at their current address as 30 (1.5% x 2 months) have moved. On December 31, only 820 will be at their current address as 180 (1.5% x 12 months) have moved. So, if you re-mailed your own mailing list just one year later you would receive up to 180 nixes. By mailing first class, some of the nixies would be forwarded to their new address, but still, most mailers would be very unhappy with a nixie rate above 5%.

Would you be upset if your mailing had 10% or 18% nixies?

You shouldn't. Why? Because nixies really are meaningless to professional mailers. What does count is the *response*. Too many amateur mailers get all wrapped up into somebody's rumor that if the list has lots of nixies, they've been ripped off. Professional mailers concentrate on the response, not on the non-response (nixies + people who didn't respond).

To put response in perspective, consider this example of two lists.

List #1 comes from your local phone book. You hired a teenager to call 1,000 people starting with the letter "A" and ask each person if their address is correct. Now you have a mailing list of 1,000 squeaky clean names as of 5:00 p.m. today. You quickly mail 1,000 recruiting letters to the Andersons, the Arnolds, and the Atkins. After one month you tally the results. First, you only had one letter come back as undeliverable, proof of your super clean list. That means 999 people received your recruiting letter. Hopefully most of them opened and read your letter.

The results? Only two people called you for more information regarding your MLM opportunity. Why? The people up and down your local streets may not be interested in extra income or multilevel marketing. But at least you *feel good* because your list was squeaky clean.

List #2 comes from a legitimate MLM enthusiasts list. Instead of paying a teenager money to verify addresses, you spent your cash for this list rental. You mail the same recruiting letter to these 1,000 MLM enthusiasts. After one month you tally the results.

First, you had 400 letters come back as undeliverable, proof that you've been ripped off and rented a dirty, nixie-filled list. That means only 600 people received your recruiting letter. Hopefully most of them opened and read your letter. The results? 56 people called you for more information regarding your MLM opportunity. Why? Because they were interested in multilevel marketing already and loved your recruiting offer.

Now, which list produced the better result? List #2 out pulled list #1 by 28 times!

So, if an amateur mailed to list #2, he would probably be fuming every time he received one of his 400 nixies. He'd gripe and threaten to sue the list renter. He'd demand restitution and an apology from the list renter's mother. Plus, the amateur would never rent a list from the list renter again. Never mind the results. It's the nixies that count.

A professional mailer would quickly re-order names from the list renter. Professional mailers only worry about the 56 responses. The other 944 people are meaningless. It doesn't matter if they didn't want the offer or never received the offer.

Only the 56 responses matter.

Who is on the list is more important than how accurate is the list. In list #1, the 1,000 names could have been broken down into the following categories:

125	happy with their jobs
250	unhappy with their jobs but are too conservative to change
300	just like to sit at home and watch cable TV
100	don't bother to read their mail if it isn't a bill
100	think multilevel would require effort (a definite no-no)
100	don't think your letter was interesting
23	couldn't read
2	**responded**

In list #2, the 1,000 names could have been broken down into the following categories:

400	no longer lived at the address you mailed
400	didn't think your letter was interesting
100	didn't trust you or your offer
44	were looking for an opportunity, but yours didn't fit their criteria
56	**responded**

It's pretty obvious that the #1 criteria in list selection is *who* is on the list. The nixie ratio is meaningless.

"Nixies are bad," sounds like a neat rule to successful mailings, but it's only a myth. *Results* make the final scorecard.

"THIS IS 1990, MAN...DON'T YOU HAVE SOMETHING BIGGER THAN A LOUSY FIVE-SPOT?"

Myth #2
Mail to fresh, hotline names only

After digesting Myth #1, it's easy to see that fresh recent names cannot possibly be as important as who is on the list. Newborn babies are fresh, new, hot names that haven't been saturated with mail offers. Guess what? If you think you've found a hot list when someone tells you he has fresh names that have never been mailed, it could be from the maternity ward of General Hospital. Fresh names are only of secondary importance.

And, since when does brand-new mean better? Many list brokers want to sell you their hotline lists at a very premium price. Hotline generally means buyers within the last 30 days. Your questions should be:

"Buyers of what?"

"What ad did they respond to?"

"What do you know about these people?"

Sure, these are hot buyers, recent buyers, but who are they really?

Maybe these hotline buyers were ex-convicts who answered the following ad:

Just Paroled For Mail Fraud?

New book describes semi-legal way to earn extra money by mail order. Must have served a minimum of three years. Only $10. Please, only cashier's checks or money orders. No personal checks accepted.

Now we know the following:

First, they are hotline buyers of a book on earning extra income. They are not targeted multilevel distributors with experience.

Second, the ad they responded to attracted a high percentage of con men, not the profile we are looking to lead our multilevel groups.

Third, most of the respondents spent the last few years in prison. They may not have a natural warm market to network their opportunity.

So, hotline is meaningless *unless* you have a list of qualified prospects. Then, if you have a choice, hotline is usually worth the extra investment.

But are recent, hot, and new that important even to a qualified list?

Consider this. A bored grocery clerk reads the trash tabloid at his register station. While reading, he sees an ad that catches his attention. The ad reads:

Bored? Hate your job?
Retire in 60 days with our hot MLM program.
Call 000-000-0000 for your free information pack.

What is the bored grocery clerk's reaction when he receives his opportunity pack in the mail?

"Yikes! This may require work, sales, meetings, training, and more! I just wanted to retire."

He throws the packet in the trash and goes back to watching infomercials on cable TV.

The advertiser sells his name to a list broker as a hotline prospect, someone who inquired or bought money-making information within the last 30 days. Is this bored grocery clerk a qualified prospect? Maybe. Is he recent and hot? Well, at least he is recent.

Now, compare that hotline prospect with this old prospect.

A multilevel distributor works diligently for three years building his multilevel marketing organization. He gives meetings, trainings, and has the respect of his downline and peers. After some soul searching, he retires from the multilevel marketing career and becomes a missionary in Zaire for two years. Upon his return, he decides to go back to multilevel marketing to earn a living.

His name is two years old.

Which prospect would you like your recruiting letter to reach? The hotline bored grocery clerk or the multilevel professional who is looking for an opportunity now?

Pretty obvious. Now that doesn't mean that two-year old mailing lists are better. It only illustrates that there are plenty of highly qualified prospects who are not hotline prospects.

So, consider mailing to the best-qualified names available, regardless how old they are.

Myth #3
The 2% myth

It's like an old wives' tale. Have you ever heard this saying?

"You have to have a 2% return on your mailing or your mailing list is no good, because the average return is 2%."

What's average? What is the offer? Who came up with this average? Is average the only way to mail?

It's easy to disprove the 2% myth. Imagine these scenarios:

Scenario #1: You rent a hot list of quality multilevel marketers. You mail a 17th generation photocopy of a hand-written offer for your MLM opportunity. Because it was a quality list, most recipients will take a quick glance and file your mail in the local trash can. If you didn't care enough to make your offer readable, they won't care enough to completely read it. You'll probably get no response. So, because you got less than the 2% "average" response expected, does that mean your list was worthless?

Scenario #2: You rent the same hot list of quality multilevel marketers. You send a well-written offer with a $5 bill stapled to your cover letter. You close your letter by saying, "There's more where that $5 came from. Give me a call on my 800 number now!" Do you think you would get more than a 2% response? One distributor received almost a 35% response with only a single dollar bill stapled. So, could your offer affect your response rate above the so-called "average" of 2%?

Scenario #3: You rent the same hot list of quality multilevel marketers. You send an eight-page letter in micro type. In your letter you explain that you are only looking for former Texans, who have $10,000 to invest, who have Wednesday afternoons off, and presently have a J.C. Penney credit card. Your response may only be 1/2 of 1%. Very low, but you only wanted response from a certain defined group. Would your mailing be a failure because you wanted to locate only one or two highly defined individuals? No. In fact, you could care less about an "average" 2% return. You just want to locate one or two special people.

Scenario #4: You rent the same hot list of quality multilevel marketers. Your offer states that you only will accept phone calls from people willing to give you $100,000 for your special MLM success plan. Would you be heartbroken with only a 1% response?

The truth is: A 2% response is meaningless. Your offer controls your response. You can produce a smaller or larger response by adjusting your offer. This assumes that you are working with a qualified mailing list. Because, after the mailing list selection, your offer is the next most important part of your mailing.

You cannot completely control the mailing list. Someone provides the list to you. However, you can completely control the offer. You can write the cover letter, give free premiums, offer fast response and terrific benefits in your offer. Or, you can make the offer so selective, that only one or two will respond. The offer is your responsibility.

Let's illustrate with an example. Imagine an amateur MLMer sends out his offer to 100 people. His response? Only one person contacted him for additional information. The amateur MLM mailer shouts, "I only got a 1% response! The mailing list I rented was no good. It's nonresponsive. Only a 2% response is acceptable."

Was it the fault of the mailing list or of the offer? Is it possible the recipients were responsive, but didn't like the offer they received in the mail? Let's change the offer and see if we can get a larger response.

The new offer to the 100 names in the mailing list will go like this:

"If you call me within the next 24 hours for additional information, I'll send you $100 in cold, hard cash."

You could expect almost 100 responses to that offer.

Or, what if we mailed this offer to the 100 names in the mailing list?

"If you send me $100, I'll send you some additional information."

Our response would be underwhelming.

As we can see, there is no such thing as an *average response*. Your response will be a factor of:

1. *Your mailing list.*

The more focused your target audience, the better. Questions you should ask are:

"How recent are the names?"

"Are they really MLM participants or casual observers?"

"Do they still like MLM, or have they sworn off part-time entrepreneurial ventures?"

"Are these MLMers open-minded, or are they married to their present program?"

"Are they responsive?"

"What types of programs have they worked?"

"What are they looking for?"

"When was the last time this list was rented? What were the results?"

"What are these prospects looking for?"

"When was the last time this list was cleaned?"

"Are they true MLMers or just opportunity seekers who bought a get-rich-quick book in 1983?"

Can you get the answers to all these questions? Can you get a perfect list? Probably not. Are all these questions important? Maybe not. However, they can be a guideline to sort out obviously rotten lists.

2. *Your offer.*

If you are targeting the right people, your offer will be the next most important factor.

Your offer can control the response rate from a low of 0% to a high of 100%. So, what does a 2% return have to do with anything? Nothing. It's just a myth passed on by a few philosophers from the local bar.

As another example, did you ever get a mailing advertising a certain brand of automobile? Think about it. Do you think the automobile manufacturer got a 2% response? If he mailed out 100,000 mailers in your community, do you think 2,000 people rushed to the local dealership to buy a new automobile? Of course not. If the manufacturer got only 100 people to buy a new car, that would be incredibly successful. That's only a 1/10 of 1% return. Offers of larger dollar amounts expect a smaller percentage return. It's okay. The offer at 1/10 of 1% can still be a winner.

Well, if we can control the response from 0% to 100%, what response do we want?

First, we don't want a 0% response. That represents a 100% waste in postage, printing, and effort.

Second, we don't want a 100% response. By bribing people to call for a $100 reward, we would have mostly unqualified gold diggers who are not interested in our opportunity, but only interested in collecting the $100 reward.

We must be more selective. We want our offer to appeal to a select few workers who are willing to work our business opportunity. So, we must make our offer's appeal good enough to attract our preferred prospects, yet not attractive enough to appeal to curiosity seekers.

If we are smart, we will realize that the quality of the person responding is more important than the number of people who respond. Remember how professionals mail for leaders, not distributors? Maybe you are only looking for that one good person to mentor. Since one leader can be worth 100 distributors, you will be excited with a 1% return if that means you locate a leader with only 100 mailings. Distributors come and go, but leaders are money in the bank.

What if you made your offer too lucrative? Let's say your offer promised:

- Free sign-up.
- No distributor kit to buy.
- No products to purchase.
- No recruiting required.
- No meetings to attend.
- No retailing required.
- Your sponsor will do all the work.
- Big bonus checks for everybody.

Sure, your response will be higher, but who did you attract? People with a distributor mentality that expect instant riches with little or no effort. The rest of your career will consist of hand-holding, babysitting, educating, motivating, and pleading with your new recruit to do something. Not a pretty picture. Getting a new recruit with a distributor mentality (free money, get-rich-quick, no effort) means they want you to give them a free ride to wealth.

What else makes a bad offer? Simply talk about how wonderful the company is, how wonderful you are, how wonderful the founder is, how wonderful the opportunity is, etc. While wonderful makes us feel good, the prospect wants to know a simple question:

"What's in it for me?"

Surely the prospect is happy that you feel wonderful, but his number one concern is how he can benefit from your offer. So, why not sell your prospect on what a terrific deal you are offering him?

Could you offer a free cassette or video for your prospect's evaluation? Would you charge a small fee to eliminate curiosity seekers?

Could you offer a free or low-cost sample or trial period of your product?

Could you include testimonials and stories of how other distributors are building their business and share their secrets of success?

Could you offer free or low-cost specialty training, consulting, co-op recruiting services, or special retail methods?

Could you offer to be his full-time employee for three or four weeks to get your prospect off to a fast start?

In other words, your prospect wants to see you meet him halfway on your offer. Selfish offers such as . . .

"I'm making a lot of money. So, you should send me money for the distributor kit and product. You're on your own, so go for it. The opportunity is there, go make me some bonuses,"

. . . won't impress the stranger who receives your mailing. If you rent a list, pay for printing, pay for postage, and invest your labor, you will want to make your offer as impressive as possible.

3. Appearance and presentation.

A lousy, smudged, amateur mailing piece will still pull response if you go to the right people with the right offer. While appearance and presentation are the least important of these three factors, the better your appearance and presentation, the better your results. Faded photocopies and copies with coffee spills leave a bad impression of your sales letter and offer.

To show why the list and offer is more important than the presentation, consider this example:

You send a beautiful four-color prospectus complete with catalog and credibility folio as your presentation piece for your MLM opportunity. Unfortunately, your mailing list consists of Mongolian prison inmates who can't read English, have no American money for a distributor kit, and are looking for an offer to get out of prison, not an offer to market high-end designer vitamins.

The presentation is great, however, the list and offer are not appropriate and your response will be poor.

Conversely, if you mail a simple handwritten sales letter that offers your full-time commitment to your prospect's success, and you mail it to a hot list of MLMers who are looking for an opportunity, your results will be better.

4. Tips.

Your MLM distributors will love to do their recruiting by mail. Why? There is no rejection. They only get the "yeses" as replies. They won't face snickering relatives, friends, and co-workers who will delight in criticism of their dreams. Plus, recruiting by mail theoretically offers unlimited contacts and unlimited results because it is not limited to personal appearances and personal presentations. It looks like the easy, painless way to riches.

Of course, it's not. But if your downline insists on mailing for new recruits, teach them to mail for leaders and forget the imaginary 2% response.

Teach your downliners that they can control their response easily by using common sense techniques. Here are just a few.

1. An 800 number will generally increase response. Do you want to make it easy for your prospect to respond, or do you want only those with enough interest to call at their expense? An 800 number makes it easy for instant response, but will the extra expense be worth it?

2. Offer a special premium. Many prospects will be interested in a book, printed report or cassette tape that gives valuable information. The premium may appear valuable enough to motivate the prospect to respond to your offer. A free set of the Encyclopedia Britannica will obviously induce a higher response than a $1 cassette tape with tips on selling. What can you afford to send? How selective do you want your response?

3. Some people staple a $1 bill to their cover letter. They suggest this shows how committed they will be to the responding prospect. A $100 bill will increase the response. A penny will decrease the response. Asking prospects for $10 will reduce the response. How selective do you want to be?

4. Offer a product or a product sample. If your product is the number one motivator for new recruits, feature the product. Many products are light, inexpensive, and can show instant results in taste, performance, or other criteria. You could send a cookie or diet shake pack for the prospect to taste. You could send a gas treatment sample or enough laundry detergent for one or two loads. If your prospect takes the time to ask to try the product, certainly he is a more qualified prospect.

5. Follow up your mailings with a phone call. Professional mailers report up to a 70% increase in response by simply following up with a phone call. Possibly the prospect was interested but lost your phone number. Or, when the prospect sees that you care enough to follow up, he thinks, "I want a sponsor like you. You really care." Or, maybe the prospect just put your offer aside and forgot about it. Your phone call renewed his interest. How much time do you have for follow-up phone calls? Do you like working on the phone? Would you rather work only with the hottest prospects who take the time to call you?

6. Offer a money-back guarantee. If the prospect does not like the information pack you send him, offer a money-back guarantee. Or better yet, offer a double-your-money-back guarantee. If you want a larger response, offer to buy your prospect a new home if your information pack is not everything he wants in a business opportunity. Drastic, but effective. Your guarantee can greatly affect your response, so use with discretion.

The list of response controls is endless. The professional MLM mailer knows that he can control the response by adjusting his offer. And since the professional MLM mailer is in control, his offer targets leaders, not distributors.

Myth #4
The saturation myth

Should you remail a list 30 or 60 days later?

Should you rent a qualified list that has just been rented for another offer?

Are all the quality multilevel names saturated from previous mailings?

Imagine you picked up the Saturday morning paper. Would you start by reading the automobile classified section? No, because you probably don't need a car today.

Would you look at the automobile classified section the next day or the next? No. If you aren't interested in a car, you don't bother to read the offers. You'll only read the automobile section when you are interested in acquiring an automobile.

Prospects are the same. They'll only seriously consider your offer if they are presently in the market for another part-time or full-time income. Let's look at the average prospect. We'll call him John.

John graduates from college. He knows that all he has to do to be successful is to work diligently for five or six months with a large corporation. They'll immediately recognize his immense talent and promote him to president with lucrative retirement benefits. Will John be interested in your offer at this time of his life?

Six months later John still is at the bottom of the organization. However, he falls in love with a co-worker and they spend the next year in a whirlwind romance and make wedding plans. Will John be interested in your offer at this time of his life?

A year later, John has an enormous mortgage, two cars, and his spouse quits work to be at home with their first child. John still is at the bottom of his organization. Will John be interested in your offer at this time of his life?

For the next several years John changes jobs, has additional children, moves, buys different automobiles, gets fired, gets hired, and his life constantly changes. At certain times John will be looking for an opportunity, while other times he'll be focused on his present daily situation. The question is:

On what day did your offer arrive in John's mailbox?

Almost everyone is a prospect sometime during his life. However, he won't be a prospect *every day* of his life.

So, should you remail your prospect list at certain intervals? Should you rerun your ad?

Yes!

Simply look how your local car dealer prospects. If he runs an ad the first week of the month, he may receive 50 prospects. When he reruns that very same ad the following week, again he'll get 50 prospects. When he reruns that very same ad the following week, he'll get 50 more prospects.

And none of these prospects are the same people!

Each week old prospects dropped out of the market and new prospects entered the market. Car dealers call this the moving parade, a constant flow of new prospects passing by.

So, can your market be saturated with no opportunity for success? Unlikely.

There will always be these two groups:

First, the people who constantly change from qualified prospect to unqualified prospect throughout their lives.

Second, the moving parade of prospects who pass through your area of influence (mailing or advertising).

MLM leaders by mail

There are two types of people in MLM:

1. Those who have more money than time, and

2. Those who have more time than money.

If you have more money than time, you can simply hire a full-time copywriter, direct mail specialist, pay a mailing house, and buy yourself a multilevel business. This section isn't for you.

In fact, if you have more money than time, you're probably relaxing on a beach in Tahiti and have no interest in recruiting, training, and building a multilevel business.

The following chapters are for those of us who have more time than money and wish to supplement our local efforts by locating, training, and building multilevel leaders by mail.

Anyone can purchase mailing lists, postage, and mail multilevel offers. The trick is to perform your mailing at a profit. Most multilevelers are in the business to make a profit, not to break even or lose money on mailing campaigns.

So, if you are going to spend money mailing your offers, here are a few quick and easy ways to consistently profit from your recruiting by mail efforts.

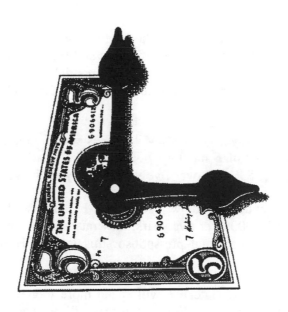

The file
drawer method

To appreciate this method fully, you must first determine the value of a good first level MLM leader. How much is he worth? Maybe $100 a month? $500 a month? Or even $5,000 a month to your regular monthly bonus check?

Let's say a good MLM leader is worth $500 a month to your regular monthly bonus check. That's $6,000 a year. Or, $30,000 over five years. Pretty exciting, eh?

Now that we know a good MLM leader can be worth up to $30,000 over five years, how much are we willing to spend to locate and pre-sponsor this leader? How about $20?

Of course, later we will spend more money developing and training this leader, but that will be financed from the bonuses we earn from the leader. For now, we are interested in locating and pre-sponsoring our next great MLM leader.

Here's one way to do it.

First, we look through all the ad sheets, junk mail, ridiculous solicitations and loser, misguided advertisements. We know these offers have little value, **but the people promoting them have a sincere desire to be successful.** Plus, these entrepreneurs willingly spend money on advertising to promote their business. We have located good people with lousy offers.

Next, we write a personal letter to these entrepreneurs. What do we say? We can tell them we are also an entrepreneur and share a common interest. We can give them hints or tips on how we are following up our mail leads. We can pass on our favorite advertising ideas. Maybe even tell our fellow entrepreneur which publications seem to work best and which ones to avoid. In other words, we want to be a friend.

If you mail out enough letters, some entrepreneurs will definitely value networking with you. You haven't asked for anything. You haven't shoved your MLM opportunity down their throat. You just gave free help without asking anything in return.

As you continue to correspond, put all your letters in a folder. Now is the time you'll need that file cabinet. As you build up a business relationship and friendship, you now have a super motivated prospect for your opportunity, if and when he stops promoting his offer.

Think of it this way. If you became discouraged with your present entrepreneurial effort, where would you look next? To a stranger? Or, to a trusted friend that you have been corresponding with for six months or a year?

Seems obvious, doesn't it?

How many entrepreneurs should you correspond with at a time? Why not shoot for 100? Maybe you can start small with five or ten, but definitely set a higher goal, such as 50 or 100. That's why you'll need a file cabinet.

Not everyone you write to will want to be your pen pal. And, not every person you correspond with will join your MLM program. But, some will. It's simply a matter of having enough entrepreneurs in your active correspondence file.

What about those 90-95% of entrepreneurs that you correspond with who don't join your program? They become good friends and there's nothing wrong with that. How many of your acquaintances can brag that they have 50 good friends?

This mailing program won't work overnight. It takes time. But, if you start today, next year could be a MLM winner. By the way, your average cost for this whole program is only about $20.

Handwritten letters

Do handwritten letters work? Yes!

Low volume, handwritten prospecting letters pull up to ten times better than photocopied or printed form letters. If we invest in postage, why not get the best results by handwriting our prospecting letter?

Imagine what happens when your prospect receives a handwritten letter. He has to read it! Why? Because there may be a personal message in there that could be important to him. There could be juicy gossip that he must know. You might mention some information about people he knows. Almost everyone will read a personalized, handwritten letter.

Form letters, even graphically impressive on high-gloss paper, will never pull as well as when you are talking personally with your prospect. Plus, form letters can easily be pitched into the wastebasket. Why should the prospect bother with your advertisement when he has more important things to do with his time — such as reading a personalized, handwritten letter.

To make a handwritten letter work, it must be truly handwritten. You can't photocopy your handwritten letter and simply pen in the person's name. The entire letter must be original.

Is that a problem? Yes. Handwritten, personalized letters take 10 or 15 minutes to write. That limits the number of prospecting letters we can mail.

It's easier to make a form letter, print thousands of copies, and mail to some rented list, but that costs big money and the results are disappointing. If a form letter pulls 1% response, the same letter could pull up to 10% if handwritten. So, if we are on a limited budget, the hand-written, personalized letter will give us up to 10 times the return for the same postage and printing investment.

Now, let's say we really do have more time than money. How can we and our downlines utilize the hand-written prospecting letter approach?

How about a goal of writing just one handwritten, personalized letter a day? That's a 10- or 15-minute investment in your business. To make our response even better, we'll write these letters to people we know. Aunts, uncles, relatives, former classmates, and casual acquaintances will be thrilled to receive a letter from us. They'll read it eagerly. Some will share our excitement for our business opportunity, some won't. But almost all will read our letter!

If we write one letter a day, every day, at the end of one year we will have sent 365 handwritten, personalized letters to someone we know or have casually met. That could translate into quite a few presentations and new distributors. And, if our downline is doing the same, our organization growth would be spectacular. It's almost impossible to have poor results. (Hermits, con artists, and sleazy, high-pressure, family outcasts should not use this method.)

If penmanship is a problem, get somebody who can write legibly for you. For instance, a husband-wife team might do this. If the wife is better at handwriting, the husband could help with the laundry, household chores, or bookkeeping duties for 15 minutes, while his wife writes the letter-of-the-day. If the husband had better handwriting, the wife could sit in front of the TV and manipulate the remote control for 15 minutes while the husband writes the letter-of-the-day. By helping with the other's duties for 15 minutes, the person with the poor penmanship can still be an integral part of the handwritten, personalized, prospecting letter campaign.

The bottom line is that for only a few cents a day in postage, any MLM distributor can have an effective mail prospecting campaign.

Piggy-back your opportunity

Some innovative MLMers use a mail order offer to pay for their mail prospecting efforts. In other words, they run a mail order business and send their MLM opportunity to their customers. Here's an example of this technique.

Our innovative MLMer might run the following ad:

How To Have A Positive Attitude. Our 45-minute cassette tape will change your life. Simply play this cassette once a day, for 30 days, and we guarantee you will have a positive attitude. Send $8.95 to Innovative MLMer, 123 Main St., Hometown, U.S.A. **Plus,** if you act now, we'll include full information on a unique business opportunity that's perfect for positive thinkers.

If the cassette tape can be inexpensively produced, and the innovative MLMer can place advertising effectively and inexpensively, his cassette proposition may break even or make a small profit. But, the real payoff is that his initial prospecting costs are fully paid by his mail order operation. His unique MLM opportunity information rides along free with his cassette sales. And, he reaches qualified prospects who want to change their lives.

Will all the cassette buyers become MLM distributors? No. But many will. The cassette buyers that do become distributors can provide a monthly income stream for the innovative MLM distributor.

The same technique can be used by direct mailers of mail order offers. They could state at the bottom of their sales letter or as a P.S. the following:

And, if you act now, we'll include this special FREE bonus. You will receive full details on the most explosive business opportunity of the decade. We've spent months investigating which business opportunities offer the best return with the least risk. This business opportunity requires less than $100 to get started, and the sky is the limit. This is truly the best of the best. And, you get our research recommendation and full information pack about this opportunity, absolutely FREE, with your order.

Not only will this extra bonus increase the response to the innovative MLMer's mail order offer, but again his prospecting costs are minimal. The MLM information rides along with the order to qualified prospects who are looking forward to receiving information about this unique business opportunity.

What if you're not in the mail order business? No problem. Sponsor someone who is. Simply inform the mail order operator that he could earn a continuing monthly income by including your MLM opportunity information with his fulfillment package. And, if he promotes this free bonus with his advertising or mailing, he may increase his response and earnings by receiving more orders. It's a win-win situation. The mail order operator increases his present and future earnings with little extra effort. You get a new distributor with a huge prospecting opportunity. Possibly, the mail order operator could be your next superstar.

Is this technique limited only to mail order operators? Absolutely not. Use your imagination. Who else sells a product or service that could give away your MLM opportunity information as a free bonus? Could your local health club pass out your nutrition MLM program to its health-conscious members? Could the freelance phone installer promote your long distance MLM program to his clients? Or, just let your imagination run wild.

By using a little brainpower and hard work, MLMers can promote their mail prospecting inexpensively, and sometimes for free.

Why some distributors make big bucks every month in multilevel

Why do some distributors receive big checks for a few months, but watch their income plummet in the following months even though they are working just as hard?

Why do some distributors never make a bonus check over $100?

I really thought about this hard after a good friend came to me. We hadn't seen each other for about six or seven years. He had been in one hot new opportunity after another; in fact, by his own count, over 30 great opportunities in the last six years. Almost all of them failed, and his group failed completely in each opportunity.

He said, "If all the time and effort I put into these 30 companies were focused on just one company, I'd be at the top commission and bonus earning level of that single company. Instead, I have nothing to show for my six years of work.

"In every program, I invested in a new distributor kit, in literature, in advertising, in product inventory, in training and meeting rooms, in air travel, in long distance phone calls, etc., only to have the opportunity fail me before I earned a big enough bonus check to ever break even. All my gross earnings paid for my repetitive start-up costs. I know now that you have to limit your start-up costs to only one opportunity, build a group, and then earn your profit on the subsequent months' bonus checks. You can't make a living convincing your contacts to join the next new multilevel deal of the month and then apologizing to them every 30 or 60 days. My warm contacts became my cold contacts after I had churned them through three or four programs."

I thought, "He's right. It's better to be at the top bonus and commission level of one company than at the bottom commission and bonus level of 10 companies."

So why do distributors work several programs simultaneously? To protect their income when some of their programs go bankrupt or suspend operations. They have a point when they say, "I would rather have a small bonus check from several multilevel companies than one big check from one company. That way if my single program goes bankrupt, I won't lose my whole check."

So these distributors put their effort into start-up expenses and investments into several multilevel programs. Do I agree? No.

My opinion (my valued opinion plus 25¢ = a quarter) is that, instead of investing all your time and money joining several multilevel programs — spend that same amount of time and money searching for the one stable program to which you can devote 100% of your efforts.

J. Paul Getty said the secret to his riches was that he put all his eggs in one basket, and then watched the basket.

What kinds of benefits can you expect from focusing on one company?

First, you can earn more money. Instead of being at the bottom bonus level of ten companies (because you can only dedicate a small portion of your time to each), you can concentrate your efforts to be at the top bonus level of one company. Believe me, getting paid three or four times as much for the same work at the top bonus level makes more sense than tiny checks from 10 companies that barely cover the monthly product purchase requirement.

Second, you can build a focused, goal-oriented group, instead of a fragmented downline going in different directions. If 25% of your group is trying to recruit a different 25% of your group into another program, there are going to be some unhappy sponsors and upline distributors in your organization. Some of your leaders will resent that you introduced certain programs that deflected their downline's direction. When you start messing with your downline's pocketbooks, you're heading for some major dropout activity.

Third, your overhead will be lower when you work only one program. Your overhead in each program does not stop at just the entry fee, distributor kit, training and sales aids, meeting rooms, postage, and telephone charges. You also have a monthly purchase and sales quota in most programs. Of course you can join only the companies with no quotas, but your overrides will be on downline distributors who are meeting the minimum, no-quota requirements. Any bonus percentage of no volume equals no bonus check.

Fourth, you'll be setting a good downline example. Let's say you're working on Program A and Program B. Your first level who is working Program B says to you, "Since you work two programs, I think I will too. So, I'm joining a new program, Program C. I know you're not involved in Program C, but I like it and will be putting 50% of my effort towards it. By the way, you should expect a 50% reduction in my Program B activity."

How do you feel when your bonus override is cut 50% because your first level emulates your multiple program activity? Sure, you could join Program C and hope your first level will sign up under you again, but how many programs can you join? You can't join every program your downline distributors get interested in. And besides, won't they want to sign you up as their first level in the new programs? They'll say, "Since I'm making you money in Program A, why don't you sign up under me in Program C? Fair enough?"

Fifth, you won't have to listen to other distributors say, "Oh, but why don't you join this program? It will complement what you are doing now." So let's say you're working a diet program. Gee, your downline uses the telephone, so why not get them involved in a long distance telephone service? Might as well be making a commission and bonus every time they call. Hmmm, they take baths too. Better join that new cleaner program. Your downline might take a vacation once a year — so better sign them all up in a travel program. Dieters need extra nutrition so why not get involved in a broad-line nutritional program? The cosmetic program will make everyone look pretty. The mortgage program will help any downliners who might be thinking of buying a home. Everyone drives a car and there's this terrific little multilevel company that sells only gas additives. Gee, come to think of it, almost half the multilevel programs in existence could be seen as complementary additions for your present downline.

Complementary programs sound great in theory, but the lack of focus keeps the core program from growing. Just look at a successful retail business. Let's take a clothing store. Should it open a travel agency just because some of its customers may travel? Or a bank? Or an automobile manufacturing plant? A telephone company? Of course not! All these businesses would be too hard to manage and the clothing store's sales would certainly suffer.

There are many great businesses and programs. You just have to pick the one that's best for you — and make sure you work that program. Which program is best for you? Your mother-in-law can't tell you, your state's governor can't tell you, nor can your best friend tell you. Only you can decide which program fits your interest, your personality, your life.

How small, plodding, blue-collar, untalented people make it big in MLM

Sure, it's easy to make big money in MLM. All you have to do is be a great salesman, have lots of contacts, be well-connected in your home town, or know a few self-starting, super motivated leaders.

And then, there's the rest of us. How do we reach MLM greatness without the connections and talent of those pedestal-bound, chest-pounding, egomaniac MLM super-promoters?

The answer? **Persistence.** (Luck works too, but I haven't figured out how to perform luck on a consistent basis.)

MLM is a neat business because it will wait for you to be successful. Most businesses require you to be a success immediately to cover the mandatory overhead and investment. In MLM, you can plod along at your own pace and gradually build your business. We don't have to cover overhead and expenses while we're learning.

Even if it takes you one, two, or even several years to build your MLM business, you can be successful if you just give it enough time. Near the end of my second year in MLM, I took stock of my progress. At that moment, I had zero distributors and zero retail customers. Other than those two drawbacks, I was doing pretty well.

I knew my company's product line inside and out.

I had attended every possible opportunity presentation, training meeting, rally, seminar and convention.

I had tested and proven hundreds of sponsoring techniques that didn't work.

From repeated failures, I had perfected my recruiting presentation.

I knew my business inside and out. I just wasn't very good at it. It was only after my first two years in MLM that I finally made monetary progress.

Do I recommend everyone to start slow like I did? No. But I do recommend that if your progress doesn't meet your expectations, hang in there. The longer you work your business, the more good things can happen to you. *There's no time limit* to be successful in MLM. You just have to hang in there long enough to succeed.

Now, not quitting isn't enough. Don't stay home and collect your company's monthly newsletter. Effort is required. It doesn't have to be competent effort, just some effort on your part. And, you have to pick a company that *will be around* when you finally make your business a success.

See, if you work a little bit each day, each day you'll be getting a little closer to your success goal with your MLM company. But, if you switch companies every 90 days, then every 90 days you are starting over from "square one."

You can't make your efforts accumulate if you are constantly starting over. So, pick a company that you wish to succeed at — and then focus your work to reach the top of that company.

Don't pick 10 different companies and wait to see which company will do the best after several months of inactivity or scattered effort. Success requires a lot of effort. And if you can only give a company one tenth of your part-time effort, don't blame the ten companies for your failure. You do have to put something into your business in order to reap rewards in return.

Even though there are many good MLM companies, you can't work all of them. There are many good Fortune 500 companies, and you can't work for all of them either. Do you really think General Motors would promote you to a top vice-president position if they had to time-share your time and effort with Ford, Chrysler, Honda, Toyota, Subaru, and Nissan? An hour a day at each auto company's plant won't get you to the top.

There are many good people in this world, but you can't be married to all of them. You have to choose just one.

An experienced multileveler once said, "I'd rather be at the top bonus level in one company than at the bottom bonus level in ten companies."

So, put your MLM focus on *one* opportunity and use each day to build on your success.

Ninja mail

The famous Ninja recruiters use stealth, cunning, and planning to crush their mail competition. True Ninja recruiters hit their feeble competition where they aren't looking. And it's so easy. All you have to do to be a Ninja recruiter is to "zig" when the competition "zags."

Don't get into the herd mentality by following the followers. Be different. Recruit where your competition doesn't recruit. Recruit when the competition isn't. If you only follow the crowd, the view in front gets pretty boring.

Here is a story to illustrate how the herd of mediocrity thinks.

Once upon a time there was a society of blind people. Everyone was blind. A one-eyed stranger wandered into town. Because he had vision in his one eye, he looked at things differently. Soon, the townspeople called him "the oddball." The stranger tried to have empathy with the townspeople. He even tried to see things from their perspective. It was no use. He couldn't fit in.

Lonely and depressed, the one-eyed man sought counseling. After listening to the one-eyed man's woes, the counselor said,

"Sir, if you would just poke your good eye out, you'd fit right in with the rest of us."

That's what the herd of mediocrity wants. They want to bring people down to their level. They don't want a change or new ideas. They simply wander in whatever direction the crowd shuffles.

However, Ninja recruiters seek out the best opportunities to ply their trade. When the masses are mailing photocopied, boring offers, the Ninja recruiter is mailing sharp, focused, personalized letters. When the masses stop their mailings, the Ninja recruiter begins a larger mailing campaign. When the masses go south, the Ninja recruiter goes north.

For example, when is the worst time to search for new MLM leaders? How about summers and holidays? Most mailers stop their mail recruiting campaigns during these periods. They don't want to waste postage. Prospects are busy outdoors with their families enjoying summer. And, it is hard for prospects to concentrate on starting a new MLM business during the Christmas holidays. The average mailer prefers to save his postage and promotional monies for when his prospects will be more open to his opportunity.

But, who decided that prospects weren't interested during the summer and holidays? Ask most mailers this question and they shrug their shoulders. They don't know. Somebody told them not to mail during these periods, but they can't remember who.

Who told these mailers to stop mailing? Their competition.

The competition prefers that their mailing arrives without other competing offers. They want to stand out as the only offer the prospect receives that day.

Could this be true? Let's look at what happens to the average prospect over the summer months.

Mr. Prospect does not receive 90 days of uninterrupted vacation. He works the entire summer with the possibility of two weeks vacation. The rest of the summer is "business as usual." Does the mortgage payment still go on? Do the charge card companies still send statements? Does the prospect continue to hate his job?

Yes.

Not to offer the prospect an opportunity during the summer months is to assume that the prospect becomes a brain-dead badminton player for 90 days and the world's economy goes on hold. That's a bad assumption.

Our prospects have needs, wants, and desires throughout the summer. If we can convince our competition to go into hiding for 90 days, that leaves the entire market to us! Our personalized mailing will stand out in the prospect's mailbox. And, our prospect will read our offer. It's either watch summer Bonanza reruns on cable TV, or investigate our exciting opportunity that can change his life.

Of course, not every prospect will take action. Some prospects will complain that it is summer. These same prospects complain that fall is bad because it's football season. And, winter is too cold. And, they always contract that dreaded spring fever. These prospects are useless 365 days a year.

What about the holidays? What happens to our prospects then?

Imagine it is the 27th of December. Aunt Fatso and her family have enjoyed their week's stay. She announces the following . . .

"Because of your wonderful hospitality, Mr. Prospect, my family and I have decided to stay an extra week. Now, let's all sit down in the living room while I re-tell you about my last gall bladder operation."

If Mr. Prospect receives your exciting MLM offer in the mail, what will he decide? Will he put your offer aside and listen to Aunt Fatso? Or, will he excuse himself from the living room and go read how your offer can change his life?

It's pretty obvious. Mr. Prospect has needs, wants, and desires during the holiday season too. And, if you deliver the only offer, you're in luck. You just have to keep convincing the competition not to mail during these "bad times."

This doesn't mean you shouldn't mail during the so-called "hot" mailing months. It only means that you will have more competition to your offer during the "hot" mailing months. During the so-called "bad" mailing times of summer and holidays, you only have to compete with some 59¢ lettuce coupons. Your personalized Ninja mailing will stand out during these times of low competition.

It's a matter of perspective

Texas and Oklahoma are bitter college football rivals. There's no middle ground.

One day a Texas football fan was driving through Oklahoma on his way to another state. (Texas football fans never drive to Oklahoma, they only drive through Oklahoma to get somewhere else.) The Texas football fan stops at an Oklahoma gas station to refuel.

A little girl walks by and suddenly is attacked by a vicious pit bull. The dog tears her dress and grabs her arm. The Texas football fan sees the screaming little girl and runs to her rescue. He grabs the pit bull and struggles valiantly. The dog tears into his flesh. Blood streams from his arm and leg. Finally, in a desperate move, the Texas football fan gets the upper hand and kills the pit bull.

A reporter for the *Oklahoma Times Newspaper* watches the drama unfold. After the pit bull is dead he approaches the Texas football fan and says:

"Wow! What a hero! This will make great headlines in tomorrow's paper. Let me take your picture and ask a few questions."

The Texas football fan wipes the blood off his arm and leg and has his picture taken.

"We'll put a great headline and story under your picture in tomorrow's paper," says the reporter. "Maybe, the headline could read, *Hero Saves Little Girl*. By the way, where are you from?"

"From Texas," says the hero.

The reporter thought for a moment and replied, "Well, since you're from Texas I guess we could change the headline to read: *Man Rescues Child*. I can kind of overlook that you're from Texas, but tell me, you at least root for the Oklahoma football team, don't you?"

The Texan replied, "No. To tell you the truth, I am a avid Texas football fan."

The reporter left to write up the story. The Texan decided to stay around for a day so he could read his headline and story in the next morning's paper.

The next morning, the Texas football fan picks up the *Oklahoma Times Newspaper* and on the front page was the headline:

Man Kills Family Pet!

It's a matter of perspective. Not everyone looks at opportunities and events the same way. While you may think you are offering a tremendous opportunity to a prospect, the prospect may see the presentation as a thinly veiled attempt to take his money.

Empathy: Identification with and understanding of another's feelings, situation, and motives.

Would you like to increase your closing percentage? Use empathy.

Would you like to increase your group's motivation? Use empathy.

Would you like to understand why people respond the way they do? Use empathy.

Great MLM leaders don't sell, they understand.

When giving a presentation, they try to present the opportunity from the prospect's point of view. If the prospect has experienced a bad situation with high-pressure salesmen, the leader gives advice and options. If the prospect is worried about his daily living expenses, the leader emphasizes the possibility of immediate part-time income. If the prospect is afraid of what his friends will say, the leader shows how the prospect can market to strangers.

To understand how effective empathy can be, imagine if a salesman used empathy to understand your point of view.

Let's say you were a prospect for a MLM opportunity. You sincerely want a part-time income, but also want quality time with your family. Compare the following two presentations:

Presentation #1

"You'll just love this MLM opportunity. You get to go to rallies, trainings, opportunity meetings, conventions, and presentations in prospects' homes and our weekly idea session. I've been in this opportunity for over a year now and I can't think of anything else. I'm doing this business 24 hours a day. You'll love it too. It will become a obsession."

Presentation #2

"You'll just love this MLM opportunity. It only takes a few hours of quality time per week. We have many successful leaders who set aside six hours a week for presentations and group building. This leaves them plenty of time to enjoy their family, friends and other activities. MLM is great because you can set your own hours."

Since your goal was part-time income and quality time, which presentation would appeal to you? It's easy to see that Presentation #2 had empathy while Presentation #1 only showed self-interest.

Empathy works for recruiting presentations, but it works even better when trying to develop MLM leaders. Let's say you want to develop Mary into your next superstar leader.

Why not find out a little about Mary's background? Is she conservative or liberal? Does she want to earn big money fast, or is she willing to build long-term? Does she want an aggressive upline sponsor and an aggressive promotional campaign? What's happening with her personal life? Is her job fulfilling or boring?

In other words, find out what Mary really wants and help her achieve it. When the upline leader and the potential leader operate on the same frequency with the same goals and strategy, magic happens. That's why some MLM leaders can develop leaders and inspire loyalty while other MLM leaders never seem to get anyone beyond a dependent distributor level.

It's just like the *Oklahoma Times Newspaper* reporter. He saw things completely different. Succeed in MLM by seeing things through other people's eyes.

Here are four more *Big Al Recruiting Books* you'll want in your library:

#1 *Big Al Tells All, The Recruiting System (Sponsoring Magic).* This is the original Big Al classic that details the entire Big Al Recruiting System. You'll learn about:

♦ Locating and qualifying new prospects
♦ Closing before you start your presentation
♦ The magic two questions
♦ Making fear of loss work for you
♦ The dairy farm syndrome
♦ The 25-minute presentation that works
♦ Strawberries as a selling tool
♦ Ridding your organization of the ten deadly myths
♦ And much, much more

If you were to read only one Big Al book, this should be your first choice.

#2 *How To Create A Recruiting Explosion.* This book contains more advanced recruiting techniques such as:

♦ Locating the fishing hole
♦ Too good to be true
♦ The checklist close
♦ Trade show challenges
♦ Finding the best people
♦ Ad techniques
♦ Handling questions
♦ Street smarts
♦ Office problems

And, the all-time blockbuster recruiting technique, *The Stair Step Solution!*

#3 *Turbo MLM*. Accelerate your group-building with this third book in the *Big Al* Recruiting Series. Turbocharge your recruiting methods by using:

◆ The million dollar close

◆ Mail order recruiting

◆ Handling money handicaps

◆ Sorting for true leaders

◆ Tale of two winners

◆ Dangers of over training

◆ Why prospects don't join

And, the all-time super income builder: *The Presentation Ratings Game.*

#5 *Super Prospecting: Special Offers & Quick-Start Systems*. Book #5 in the *Big Al Series* describes the A.S.K. recruiting system that puts your new distributor to work in less than three minutes. This no-wait system makes recruiting easy for shy, busy, or brand new distributors. Plus, there are special sections on how to make your offers irresistible, how to get prospects to come to you, and more. It's brand new and maybe the best *Big Al* book ever published!

Volume Discounts

All *Big Al* Recruiting Books are $12.95 each. For the professional leader who wishes to take advantage of *Big Al's* surprisingly generous quantity discounts, the following schedule applies for *any combination* of his five books:

10-24	$6.95 ea.
25-49	$6.00 ea.
50-99	$5.00 ea.
100-499	$4.25 ea.
500 or more	$3.95 ea.

Feel a bit shy when approaching strangers? Would you like to turn acquaintances into hot, eager prospects? How can you approach potential prospects about your business without looking like a greedy salesman searching for a quick commission?

How To Get Rich Without Winning The Lottery, by Keith Schreiter is easy to read, easy to implement, and shows how anyone, a carpenter, a rocket scientist, a housewife, or even a lawyer (gasp!) can follow the simple principles to accumulate wealth. And the best part is that this book will show your prospects how to add network marketing to their wealth plan if they wish.

This is a gift that will build a long-term relationship. So leave a copy of this book with that cab driver who gave you good service, to that hotel employee who helped you set up your opportunity meeting, to the waitress with the million-dollar smile, and to your best friend who would like to be rich, but doesn't knew how.

Once you read this book, your life will never be the same. You'll be on the direct road to financial independence even without the help of network marketing. And because you already do network marketing, you'll be way ahead on this million-dollar road to riches. The book is so good, you won't want to give away your personal copy.

Give the books away?

Yes. These books were meant to given away as gifts that will instantly bond you with your prospect.

And the price? A little more than $1 each in quantities. About the cost of an audiocassette tape, but so much more impressive.

The proof is in the results. First, you'll personally love the book as it will quickly direct you to the most direct road to wealth. Second, you'll love the instant relationships this book creates with your prospects. Now you have something really important to talk about. And third, the book pre-sells network marketing so that your prospect is ready to take advantage of your business opportunity.

Single book	$4.00 each
2-99 books	$2.50 each
100-499 books	$1.38 each
500 –1000 books	$1.29 each
1000+ books	$1.23 each

(plus $3 S/H per order)

To order contact:

KAAS Publishing
P.O. Box 890084
Houston, TX 77289

http://www.fortunenow.com

Visa, MasterCard, Discover and American Express orders
Phone (281) 280-9800 or
Fax: (281) 486-0549

Do you want more great recruiting ideas?

Call (281) 280-9800
Fax: (281) 486-0549

Visit our website at
http://www.fortunenow.com

Or write to:

KAAS Publishing
P.O. Box 890084
Houston, TX 77289

We'll send you a **_free_** copy of our training journal with free sources and tips.